"Catastrophes"

Seeing the
Bright Side
When Life
Isn't Purrfect

ARTWORK BY
Gay Talbott Boassy

HARVEST HOUSE PUBLISHERS
Eugene, Oregon

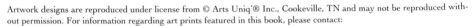

"Cat"astrophes

Text Copyright © 2000 Harvest House Publishers
Eugene, Oregon 97402

ISBN 0-7369-0389-5

Artwork designs are reproduced under license from © Arts Uniq'® Inc., Cookeville, TN and may not be reproduced without permission. For information regarding art prints featured in this book, please contact:

> Arts Uniq'
> P.O. Box 3085
> Cookeville, TN 38502
> 800/223-5020

Design and production by Garborg Design Works, Minneapolis, Minnesota

Harvest House Publishers has made every effort to trace the ownership of all poems and quotes. In the event of a question arising from the use of a poem or quote, we regret any error made and will be pleased to make the necessary correction in future editions of this book.

Scripture quotations are taken from the Holy Bible, New International Version®, Copyright © 1973, 1978, 1984 by the International Bible Society. Used by permission of Zondervan Publishing House.

Printed in China.

00 01 02 03 04 05 06 07 08 09 / PP / 10 9 8 7 6 5 4 3 2 1

Sometimes doors are closed for us, giving us no choice but to move forward. It's nice to think that our most difficult times are blessings in disguise.

ANONYMOUS

Finding the bright side of things when darkness looms can be a true test of your spirit. Don't let bumps in the road of life detour you—instead, trust them to make you stronger. Find comfort and solace in the fact that many people, both great and small, have turned some of life's toughest adversities into history's greatest triumphs.

Allow these words of encouragement to help you through tough times, inspire you to keep your chin up, and remind you that God is always on your side.

Every problem
is just an
opportunity
waiting to be
made use of.

ANONYMOUS

When you get into a tight place and everything goes against you, till it seems as though you could not hang on a minute longer, never give up then, for that is just the place and time that the tide will turn.

HARRIET BEECHER STOWE

A stumble may prevent a fall.

THOMAS FULLER

Courage does not always roar. Sometimes courage is the small, quiet voice at the end of the day saying, "I will try again tomorrow."

AUTHOR UNKNOWN

Anyone who doesn't make mistakes isn't trying hard enough.

WESS ROBERTS

6

Character cannot be developed in ease and quiet. Only through experience of trial and suffering can the soul be strengthened, vision cleared, ambition inspired, and success achieved.

HELEN KELLER

I am not afraid of tomorrow, for I have seen yesterday and I love today.

<small>WILLIAM ALLEN WHITE</small>

Necessity is the mother of taking chances.

<small>MARK TWAIN</small>

Some of the best lessons we
ever learn are learned from
past mistakes. The error of
the past is the wisdom and
success of the future.

DALE TURNER

No one ever achieved greatness
by playing it safe.

HARRY GRAY

9

Courage is grace under pressure.

ERNEST HEMINGWAY

Difficulties are meant to rouse, not discourage.

WILLIAM ELLERY CHANNING

10

If you think you can, you can. And if
you think you can't, you're right.

MARY KAY ASH

Act as if you were already happy and
that will tend to make you happy.

DALE CARNEGIE

11

Anybody can do anything
that he imagines.

HENRY FORD

Courage is very important.
Like a muscle, it is
strengthened by use.

RUTH GORDON

Always dream and shoot higher
than you know you can do.

WILLIAM FAULKNER

An optimist is a person who sees a green light everywhere, while the pessimist sees only the red stoplight.

ALBERT SCHWEITZER

Change is always
powerful. Let your
hook be always cast. In
the pool where you
least expect it,
will be a fish.

OVID

14

Do what you know best, if you're a runner, run, if you're a bell, ring.

IGNAS BERNSTEIN

Even if you're on the right track you'll get run over if you just sit there.

WILL ROGERS

Courage is contagious. When a brave man takes a stand, the spines of others are often stiffened.

BILLY GRAHAM

Far away there in the sunshine
are my highest aspirations. I
may not reach them, but
I can look up and see their
beauty, believe in them and
try to follow where they lead.

LOUISA MAY ALCOTT

Don't give in!
Make your own trail.

KATHARINE HEPBURN

I do the very best I know how — the very best I can;
and mean to keep doing so until the end.

ABRAHAM LINCOLN

I think that if you shake the
tree, you ought to be around
when the fruit falls to pick it up.

MARY CASSATT

17

It is common sense to take a method and try it. If it fails, admit it frankly and try another. But above all, try something.

FRANKLIN D. ROOSEVELT

Life is like riding a bicycle. You don't fall off unless you stop peddling.

CLAUDE PEPPER

Miracles happen to those who believe in them.

BERNARD BERENSON

Keep on going and the chances are that you will stumble on something, perhaps when you are least expecting it. I have never heard of anyone stumbling on something sitting down.

CHARLES F. KETTERING

19

© Gay Talbott Boassy

One of the things I learned the hard way was it does not pay to get discouraged. Keeping busy and making optimism a way of life can restore your faith in yourself.

LUCILLE BALL

Mistakes are part of the dues one pays for a full life.

SOPHIA LOREN

Never measure the height of a
mountain, until you have reached the
top. Then you will see how low it was.

DAG HAMMARSKJÖLD

*Life's real failure is when you
do not realize how close you were to
success when you gave up.*

ANONYMOUS

But we also rejoice in our sufferings, because we know that suffering produces perseverance.

THE BOOK OF ROMANS

Press on. Nothing in the world can take the place of persistence.

RAY A. KROC

No one knows what it is that he can do until he tries.

PUBLILIUS SYRUS

Some people look at the world and say "why?" Some people look at the world and say "why not?"

GEORGE BERNARD SHAW

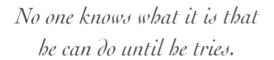

Sing when your trials are greatest,
Trust in the Lord and take heart.

FANNY CROSBY
"NEVER GIVE UP"

*Success is
getting up just
one more time
than you
fall down.*

ANONYMOUS

The art of being wise is the art of knowing what to overlook.

WILLIAM JAMES

The best way to make your dreams come true is to wake up.

PAUL VALERY

Whatever you can do, or dream
you can, begin it. Live each day
as if your life had just begun.

JOHANN WOLFGANG VON GOETHE

*Life is like a ten-speed
bike. Most of us have
gears we never use*

CHARLES SHULZ

26

*When it is dark enough,
you can see the stars.*

CHARLES A. BEARD

D̲o you not know that in a race
all the runners run, but only one
gets the prize? R̲un in such a
way as to get the prize.

THE BOOK OF I CORINTHIANS

27

You should treat all disasters as if they were trivialities, but never treat a triviality as if it were a disaster.

QUENTIN CRISP

Just pray for a tough hide and a tender heart.

RUTH GRAHAM

What the caterpillar calls
the end of the world, the
master calls a butterfly.

RICHARD BACH

*You may have to fight the
battle more than once to win it.*

MARGARET THATCHER

Trouble brings experience, and experience brings wisdom.

AUTHOR UNKNOWN

*Only those who dare to fail
greatly can ever achieve greatly.*

ROBERT F. KENNEDY

Delight yourself in the
LORD and he will give you
the desires of your heart.

THE BOOK OF PSALMS

30

Life is not meant to be easy, my child; but take courage — it can be delightful.

GEORGE BERNARD SHAW

It's never too late — in fiction or in life — to revise.

NANCY THAYER

The real glory is being
knocked to your knees and
then coming back. That's real
glory. That's the essence of it.

VINCE LOMBARDI

I always view problems as opportunities in work clothes.

HENRY KAISER

If you hear a different drummer—
dreamer, take a chance…The
road you choose to travel means
the difference in the dance.

D. MORGAN

Success is not measured by where you are in life, but the obstacles you've overcome.

BOOKER T. WASHINGTON

When someone tells you that you can't go any farther, just tell them to look behind you and see how far you've come.

LORNA PITRE

In three words I can sum up everything I've learned about life: It goes on.

ROBERT FROST

It's hard to wring my hands when I am busy rolling up my sleeves.

LINDA GERACI

Failure will never stand in the way of success if you learn from it.

HANK AARON

A mile is easiest run one step at a time.

AUTHOR UNKNOWN

36

If you get up one time more than you fall, you will make it through.

There is nothing impossible to him who will try.

ALEXANDER THE GREAT

The world belongs to those who Dream Boldly,
Care Deeply, and Work Diligently.

AUTHOR UNKNOWN

Use your weaknesses;
aspire to the strength.

LAURENCE OLIVIER

Forgetting what is
behind and straining
toward what is ahead, I
press on toward the goal
to win the prize for
which God has called
me heavenward…

THE BOOK OF PHILIPPIANS

*Making mistakes
simply means you
are learning faster.*

WESTON H. AGOR

If you can imagine it you can create it. If you can dream it, you can become it.

WILLIAM ARTHUR WARD

The eagle was once nothing but an egg.

AUTHOR UNKNOWN

Do not let what you cannot do interfere with what you can do.

JOHN WOODEN

Adversity causes some men to break; others to break records.

WILLIAM A. WARD

The winners in life think constantly in terms of I can, I will, and I am.

DENNIS WAITLEY

42

A man can succeed at almost anything
for which he has unlimited enthusiasm.

CHARLES M. SCHWAB

There is no one giant step that
does it. It's a lot of little steps.

PETER A. COHEN

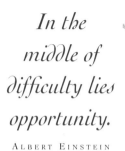

In the middle of difficulty lies opportunity.

ALBERT EINSTEIN

When life hands you lemons, make lemonade.

AUTHOR UNKNOWN

44

By persisting in your path, though you
forfeit the little, you gain the great.

RALPH WALDO EMERSON

*Keep your face to the sunshine
and you cannot see the shadow.*

HELEN KELLER

Consider it pure joy…whenever you face trials of many kinds, because you know that the testing of your faith develops perseverance.

THE BOOK OF JAMES

46

Every great work, every big accomplish-
ment, has been brought into manifestation
through holding to the vision, and often
just before the big achievement, comes
apparent failure and discouragement.

FLORENCE SCOVEL SHINN

*Courage and perseverance have
a magical talisman, before
which difficulties disappear
and obstacles vanish into air.*

JOHN QUINCY ADAMS

47

I'm proof against
that word failure.
I've seen behind it.
The only failure a
man ought to fear is
failure of cleaving to
the purpose he sees
to be best.

GEORGE ELIOT

48

If you wish to succeed in life, make perseverance your bosom friend, experience your wise counselor, caution your elder brother, and hope your guardian genius.

JOSEPH ADDISON

It's hard to beat a person who never gives up.

BABE RUTH

Faith is the victory!
Faith is the victory!
O glorious victory,
that overcomes the world.

JOHN HENRY YATES
"FAITH IS THE VICTORY"

Life is not easy for any of us. But what of that? We must have perseverance and above all confidence in ourselves. We must believe that we are gifted for something and that this thing must be attained.

MARIE CURIE

Obstacles cannot crush me; every obstacle yields to stern resolve.

LEONARDO DA VINCI

There is a strength of a quiet endurance as significant of courage as the most daring feats of prowess.

HENRY TUCKERMAN

Be happy. It is a way of being wise.

COLETTE

Vitality shows
not only in the
ability to
persist, but in
the ability to
start over.

F. Scott Fitzgerald

Experience is not what happens to a man, it's what a man does with what happens to him.

ALDOUS HUXLEY

Don't be afraid to take a big step if one is indicated. You can't cross a chasm in two small jumps.

DAVID LLOYD GEORGE

Far better it is to dare mighty things, to win glorious triumphs, even though checkered by failure, than to take rank with those poor spirits who neither enjoy much nor suffer much, because they live in the gray twilight that knows not victory nor defeat.

THEODORE ROOSEVELT

I am only one, but still I am one; I cannot do everything, but still I can do something; and because I cannot do everything I will not refuse to do the something that I can do.

EDWARD E. HALE

I learned this, at least, by my experiment: that if one advances confidently in the direction of his dreams, and endeavors to live the life which he has imagined, he will meet with a success unexpected in common hours.

HENRY DAVID THOREAU

To make our way, we must have firm resolve, persistence, tenacity. We must gear ourselves to work hard all the way. We can never let up.

RALPH BUNCHE

Ride the horse in the direction that it's going.

WERNER ERHARD

*Never accept the negative
until you have thoroughly
explored the positive.*

ANONYMOUS

No one can make
you feel inferior
without your consent.

ELEANOR ROOSEVELT

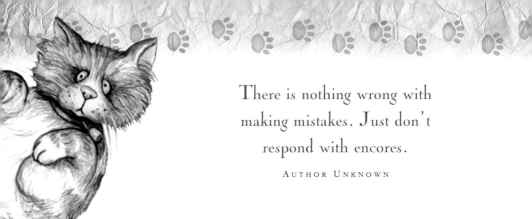

There is nothing wrong with
making mistakes. Just don't
respond with encores.

AUTHOR UNKNOWN

The greatest discovery of my generation
is that a human being can change his life
by changing his attitude of mind.

WILLIAM JAMES

You start at the
beginning, go on
until you get to the
end, then stop.

LEWIS CARROLL

*Wisdom is offtimes nearer
when we stoop than when we soar.*

WILLIAM WORDSWORTH

62

Now faith is being sure of what we hope for and certain of what we do not see.

THE BOOK OF HEBREWS

Faith is to believe what you do not yet see; the reward for this faith is to see what you believe.

ST. AUGUSTINE

We know what we are, but know not what we may be.

WILLIAM SHAKESPEARE